JESUS AND . . .

TEN SESSION OUTLINES
FOR CHILDREN

NICK HARDING

Kevin
Mayhew

First published in 1999 by
KEVIN MAYHEW LTD
Buxhall
Stowmarket
Suffolk IP14 3DJ

0 1 2 3 4 5 6 7 8 9

ISBN 1 84003 324 X
Catalogue No. 1500249

Cover design by Jonathan Stroulger
Illustrations by Simon Smith
Edited by Helen Elliot
Typesetting by Louise Selfe
Printed in Great Britain

Contents

About the author

Nick Harding grew up in Birmingham, found faith at a Baptist Church, spent student days in Devon, taught for a few years near Nottingham, and has been up to his eyes in children's and youth work ever since! He lives near Sherwood Forest with his wife and two energetic sons, loves the music of Elton John and Elgar, supports Aston Villa, is a member of the Mother's Union, and travels on buses as a hobby! He works for his local cathedral, Southwell Minster, as Schools Officer where he also runs an award-winning educational project called 'Time Travelling!' He loves preaching, which he does every Sunday at churches of most denominations and traditions. Best recent moment – being really busy with a new challenge. Worst recent moment – fluffing the first line of a 'thought for the day' on BBC local radio!

Introduction _____

- Have you ever been stuck for material, and found that the time you put aside to plan has vanished?

- Have you ever struggled to use published material because it assumes the children have good Bible knowledge?

These are problems faced by everyone who works with children, whether in church or school. The following session outlines are designed to meet your needs, with easy-to-prepare and varied material, including plenty of activity and lots for children to think about. They are aimed at children on the fringe of the church and those outside – perhaps who come to a holiday club, attend a midweek group, or go to the Christian group at school. They are intended for the 7-12 age group, but are adaptable for use with both younger and older groups. All the material here has been tried and tested over a number of years and should provide all you need to help young people with no church experience get to grips with the nature of Jesus, and ultimately his love for them.

Each outline follows the same pattern, giving a number of sections which can be used. Remember that there is probably too much for one session and you may want to miss items out or do them the following week. Other suggestions may be unsuitable for your group or facilities.

Theme

At the start of each outline is a clearly defined theme. This is to help you understand the point that the games, stories and talk suggestions are working towards.

Active game

There is at least one active game suggestion during each outline. This is provided to enable the young people to let off steam in a fun way, with a connection to the theme of the session.

Game

There is often another game which involves some of the group. Be aware that when asking for 'volunteers' you need to aim for a balance of boys and girls, able and less able, and so on.

Illustration

There are simple illustrations for a leader to act out included in some of these outlines. They introduce the theme of the session.

Quiz   Many of the outlines have a quiz suggestion to enable you to reinforce the point, or to introduce the theme. These are not meant to be too competitive and shouldn't be taken too seriously!

Discussion A vital skill to learn is the ability to express a point of view in a supportive environment. Discussion suggestions are provided to help you explore the theme and develop the children's skills at giving and receiving information.

Talk   It is sometimes necessary for you to be clear about what you want to say rather than having a discussion. Some outlines include talks, with the main points listed.

Craft   These outlines include a craft suggestion where suitable and relevant. Most children learn best by doing, so it's good to include as much activity as possible in your plans. These are kept as simple as possible, requiring a minimum of materials and equipment.

Bible input Every outline includes a Bible reference and a suggestion as to how you may want to tell the story. Remember that the children may be unfamiliar with the Bible and it should always be presented in a positive and lively manner.

Prayer   At the end of each outline is a prayer or a prayer suggestion. These vary from quiet and meditative to lively, aimed at children who are not used to praying and who may be embarrassed by it.

Memory chant Each outline includes a simple chant on the theme of that day. These could be learned, memorised, repeated each session and added to as you go along, giving all the group members some basic truths to remember.

Songs   There are suggested songs given, but don't be restricted by this list. Most of them can be found in a large number of books from various publishers including

ICC *Spring Harvest Big Book of Kids' Praise*

ICC *Kids' Praise 1995/1996/1997/1998*

ICC/Scripture Union *Everybody Praise*

HarperCollins *Junior Praise*

Kevin Mayhew *Children's Hymn Book, The Source*
SU Missions Dept. *J Team Songs*
BBC *Come and Praise, Books 1 and 2*
You may know and use much more relevant and suitable songs!

Funsheet

This is for you to photocopy and use either as part of the session or to give the children to take home and complete. It complements the session but does not have to be used at the same time. Ingredients include wordsearches, questions, puzzles, prayers, thought-starters and quizzes.

You need to add . . .

(a)   time for registration, notices, chatting, tuck shop and whatever else is a normal part of your regular meetings.

(b)   your own wisdom, energy and creativity to make these outlines work for you and your young people.

Other suggestions

- Use these outlines for a Holiday Club, decorating the room with 'J+' and using it on the publicity posters and leaflets.

- Use the chant 'J plus – Jesus and us' to a regular clapping rhythm. This helps reinforce the teaching message for the ten outlines.

- If you have limited time each week split each of the sessions into two, providing a balance of activity and quiet in each.

- Try saying 'Amen' in different ways – shouting, winding up (ameeeeeeeeen), 'I agree' or 'Hey, that's cool!'

I hope *J+ – Jesus and . . .* helps you do your job with children more effectively and I hope that through it more young people will come to know the life and love of Jesus for themselves.

With special thanks to
Alan Darlington and Clare

For all teachers who struggle

Session 1   Jesus and . . . people _____

Theme   Jesus was born as a person and understands what it is to be human. He knows all about us.

Active game   *Find the person . . .*
Ask the children to move around the room and stand by anyone they see who fulfils the description you give.
Find the person with:

- a bright shirt on
- a big smile
- long hair
- the oldest-looking face
- the coolest clothes
- a dark pair of trousers
- a watch on
- stripes on their clothes

Game   *My friend*
Ask two children who are friends to volunteer. One leaves the room while you ask the other this list of questions about him/her. Then the first child returns and tries to answer the questions with the same answer. The children then swap over and the game is repeated.

- What does your friend like to eat?
- What is your friend's favourite TV programme?
- What does your friend really hate at school?
- Has your friend got any brothers or sisters?
- Where would your friend love to go on holiday?

Talk   1 When we were all finding the person, none of us found someone who was completely identical to us.

2 Even the two friends who just played *My friend* are not the same.

3 All people are made by God and we are all different, yet God himself came to live as a person and knows what it is like for us.

Illustration   Hold a mini Christmas party whatever time of year it is! Have a few balloons, games like 'musical chairs' and 'pass the parcel', some nibbles and a few small presents. Then ask the children what they think Christmas is all about. Point out that the whole reason for Christmas is to celebrate the birth of God's son coming down to earth as a human.

Craft

You will need
- one small box (large matchbox or similar) for each child
- wrapping paper
- card
- pens and pencils

Give each child a matchbox and ask them to wrap it in Christmas wrapping paper, ensuring that one end will open. Then give them each a small piece of card on which they should write 'Jesus – everyone's best gift' and curl it up so it fits in the box.

Bible input

Luke 2:22-35

Jesus is presented to Simeon

Read this account from the Bible or tell the story in your own words, covering the points listed below. Remember that the idea of temples and presentation will not be familiar to many of the children.

- It was normal for a baby to be taken to the Temple (church) for someone to pray for them.

- Simeon was a wise old man and a messenger from God. God had spoken to him and told him to expect a special baby, who would save the world.

- When Mary and Joseph arrived at the Temple Simeon was waiting, and he took the baby in his arms.

- Simeon knew this was the child he had been waiting for, and he thanked God that at last the waiting was over and the world would be saved.

- Mary and Joseph didn't fully understand what was being said – they knew that their son was special, but had no idea how special he was!

Discussion

Ask the children why they think God sent his son Jesus to be born as a baby in a dirty, smelly stable. God sent his son, who suffered and died, so that we can get to know God better. We can never say that no one, not even God, understands the things we feel or suffer. God understands because, through his Son Jesus, he went through it all too.

Memory chant   Learn this chant this week:

Whatever I feel is nothing new
'cos Jesus lived and suffered too.

Prayer   Ask the children to repeat each line after you:

Thank you, God, that we are all different.
Thank you, God, that you know how we feel.
Thank you, Jesus, that you lived as a child and an adult.
Thank you, Jesus, that you know how we feel.

Songs   Go, tell it on the mountain
Thank you, Jesus
Live my life by faith
Any Christmas songs

1. Jesus and... People.

My Best Friend

Jesus AND Simeon

Draw a line between these pictures in the correct order...

Jesus is Born

Simeon sees Jesus

Mary and Joseph take Jesus to the synagogue

chant

Whatever I feel is nothing new, 'cos Jesus lived and suffered too!

what SIMEON said

" Jes_s wil_ _e a sig_ fr_m Go_. "

Fill in the missing letters:

Session 2 Jesus and . . . the things that worry us

Theme
Jesus is concerned about the things that trouble us, whether we think they are too big or too small for him. He will help us deal with them if we ask him.

Active game

Losing and finding
Hide several objects around the room for the children to find as they arrive. Once they have found all the objects ask them to leave the room while you hide each of these letters: W O R R Y L O S T S A D H E L P. The group should then find the letters and work together to find out what words can be formed. The words could then be used to illustrate the later discussion.

Game

The brick game
Using a foam brick, inflatable mallet or similar, play this simple word association game. A pair of children compete to win, with the child who hesitates for too long or repeats a word that has already been used being 'out' and tapped on the head or back (gently!) with the brick. Play rounds on the following subjects:

• Losing something special

• Being scared

• Things I worry about

• Being upset

Discussion
Talk about a time when you lost something of value or importance, and tell the children how you felt about it, then invite them to talk about losing things and how it makes them feel. How did they or would they go about finding the object that was lost?

Bible input
Matthew 18:10-14 or Luke 15:3-7

The Parable of the Lost Sheep

This is best told as a story, and in the example below we are looking at things from the sheep's point of view.

Charlie the sheep was part of a big family. They spent most of their time happily playing and eating in the fields. One day Charlie was bored and wanted to do some exploring, so he wandered away from the others. He walked a long way across fields, bridges and lanes, through valleys, woods and streams. He was a very long way away from the others when he began to feel hungry, and before long the sky started to get dark. It was then that Charlie realised he had no idea where he had come from or which way he should go to get back to the family. To put it bluntly, he was lost. As he thought about what to do and ran this way and that he became increasingly frightened, and finally slumped down and cried. After a while it was so dark that he could hardly see anything, and the breeze was rustling in the trees. Then he heard a noise. As he crouched down his heart pounded – was it a wolf? Could it be a lion? Would he survive? Charlie plucked up all his courage and opened his eyes, looking towards the noise. But he didn't see a wolf or a lion – instead he saw the familiar face of the shepherd coming to take him home.

Quiz

Read out the story a second time, this time slipping in some wrong words. Ask the children to go 'baaa' if they spot a word that was not in the original story, for example: Charlie the *dog* was part of a big family. They spent most of their *money* happily playing . . .

Discussion

Talk about how Charlie felt at different stages of the story. He moved from feeling bored to being brave, and then to being scared and lonely. Then ask about the things that worry or concern the children. Ask what they do when they feel like this – who do they turn to, and how do they get help? In the story the shepherd went out of his way to help Charlie. This is a similar story to one Jesus told, and he called himself the Good Shepherd. Explain to the children that when we have worries, concerns or problems Jesus is willing to be a shepherd for us, finding us and helping us when we struggle. Because he loves us he will go out of his way to help us.

Craft

You will need:

- card
- Sellotape
- cotton wool
- white material
- paper

Produce a template of a sheep, about 20 cm long. Each of the children should cut it out of cardboard, attach a stick to it, and decorate it with cotton wool, material and paper.

Charlie the Sheep

Memory chant   Teach this one this week:

Jesus cares lots when we fear.
Just shout his name – he's always near.

Prayer   Make a list of some of the things that worry or concern the children in the group. Then pray this prayer, repeating it and filling in the gaps with the children's concerns:

Thank you, Jesus, that you are a really good shepherd.
You look after us all, even when we feel . . .
Help us to ask you for help. Amen

Songs   Jesus' love is a powerful love
God loves you, he cares about you
He's got the whole world
My God is so big

fill these words on the sheep...

good
I
am
the
shepherd

Jesus said

Lost & found

find 8 Valuable things

friend
money
life
health
home

gold   hope   faith

X	H	O	P	E	T	A
U	O	Z	J	H	S	F
Q	M	O	N	E	Y	R
S	E	D	B	A	W	I
C	K	G	O	L	D	E
V	F	A	I	T	H	N
L	I	F	E	H	L	D

Chant

Jesus cares lots when we fear,
Just shout his name - he's always near!

Session 3   Jesus and . . . the way to go _____

Theme   There are a number of ways that we can choose to go in life. Jesus is willing to show us the way to go and will guide us through life.

Active game   *Blindfold obstacle relay*
Divide the children into two or three teams and arrange an obstacle course around the room. The first member of each team must lead the second, who is blindfolded, to the other side of the room giving verbal instructions. They are not allowed to touch each other. When they reach the other side of the room the blindfold is removed and they both run back. Player 1 goes to the back of the team while player 2 becomes the new guide, with player 3 blindfolded, and so on. The team to get all of its members across the room first is the winning team.

Illustration   A leader (A) arrives disguised in a hiking costume, looking confused and lost. A second leader (B) asks the first what he is doing. This dialogue or similar should then be acted out:

A. I'm looking for . . . (local landmark). I was standing near the shops when this man told me to go to the end of the road and turn left.

B. So what did you do?

A. I went to the end of the road and turned right, and ended up walking into this with you lot!

B. OK. Now listen carefully to what I tell you. Go outside onto the High Street and turn left. Keep walking until you get to the park, and it's there, on the right.

A. Thanks . . . um . . . er . . . turn right across the High Street, keep walking till it gets dark, then it's there, under the light! (He leaves, going in the wrong direction.)

Game   *Balancing act*
Get two volunteers out, and ask them to get into the following positions. They must follow the directions given by the leader. The one who does it best and balances longest is the winner:

• stand on one leg

• stand on two legs and a hand

• stand on one leg and one hand

21

- balance on your back
- balance on your bottom and one foot
- stand on both knees and hands but no feet

Discussion Lead the children into thinking about directions by bringing out the following points:

- In the blindfold relay you had to know whose instructions you were following and to do what you were told, otherwise it went wrong.

- The lost person got instructions but did not follow them. If we get good instructions we must do what they say.

Craft You will need:

- paper
- pens and pencils

Give each child a piece of paper and ask them to draw as many road signs as they can, colouring them in the correct way and writing underneath what they mean. If possible go for a short walk and look at local signs before you do this activity.

Bible input Matthew 4:24-27

The two house-builders

Tell the story as it is written in the Bible, asking for two children to act out the parts of the builders as you tell it. Alternatively, the story could be told as *The two little pigs,* mixing in the traditional fairy story with the parable!

After the story explain that Jesus told this parable so that people would understand that it is best to follow his instructions. We can know what Jesus wants us to do through leaders and others, the Bible, and prayer.

Quiz Have a number of varied lengths of wool (ranging from 5 cm to 30 cm) available in a bag. Ask the following questions of two teams, allowing the child who gives a right answer to pick a length of wool and tie it together for their team. The team with the longest piece of wool at the end is the winner.

Q. What instructions did the bad housebuilder not follow?
A. *Build on rock*

Q. Who gives us directions at school?
A. *Teachers, Form leaders . . .*

Q. Where was the lost leader trying to go?
A. *To the . . .*

Q. What is the colour of a 'stop' road sign?
A. *Red*

Q. What should we avoid building on?
A. *Sand*

Q. How do we know what Jesus wants us to do?
A. *Bible, prayer, others*

Memory chant

Learn this one this week:

Are you lost? Don't you know?
Jesus knows the way to go.

Prayer

Teach the response
'You know the way; I want to follow you'.

Thanks, Jesus.
Thank you that you have always cared about all of us.
You . . .

Thanks, Jesus.
Thank you that you know how we feel right now.
You . . .

Thanks, Jesus.
Thank you that you know what is best for us.
You . . .

Thanks, Jesus.
Thank you that you will show us the way and guide us.
You . . .

Songs

I have decided to follow Jesus
Step by step (Jesus is the living way)
Don't build your house on the sandy land
The wise man built his house upon the rock
Be bold, be strong

3. Jesus and ... the way to go.

Lost!

Fill in the expressions on these faces

A little lost

very lost

found

Signs — What do they mean?

× ! ↑ P T

TWO HOUSE BUILDERS

1. They start to build...

2. ...one house crumbles...

3. ...the other house stands firm!

Draw a cartoon strip!

Chant

Are you Lost? ✳ Don't you know? ✳ Jesus knows the way to go!

Session 4   Jesus and . . . the things we do wrong

Theme

We all go wrong and let ourselves, others and Jesus down. Jesus will forgive us when we do things wrong.

Active game

Simon says . . .

This age-old game remains popular with children of all backgrounds. Ask the children to stand in a space and do whatever you say so long as you preface it with 'Simon says'. If you do not preface it with that they should not do it. You may want to play competitively and have some children sitting out, or you may prefer to play it just for fun.

Talk

- The game was all about following instructions, and you could have been out if you had got it wrong.
- In the last session we learned that Jesus gives us instructions to follow, and shows us the way to go.
- We all go wrong, and do things which we should regret.
- Often we know that we've done something wrong because we feel guilty.

Discussion

Ask the children what things they do which are wrong. Try to help them focus on things which are real to them (fighting at school) rather than bigger things which they know to be wrong (murder, for example). Ask them how it feels if someone does something that is unkind to them or hurts them.

You may want to return to some of the suggestions from the group later, so you could write them down on a large sheet of paper while you discuss them.

Game

Yes/No challenge

Individual children must answer questions for 30 seconds without saying 'yes' or 'no'. If they do they have gone wrong and are out of the game. This is great fun, and bears repeating with the whole group if there is time.

Bible input

Luke 19:1-10

Zacchaeus

This story is best told as a promenade performance – all the group are involved in the presentation of the story and have a role to play. One person can play Jesus, another Zacchaeus, and the others become the crowd. The crowd should respond to the other characters' names as follows:

Zacchaeus   'What a nasty man!'

Jesus   'What a great man!'

At the end of the story the response to Zacchaeus' name needs to change to 'What a changed man!' to reinforce the change in his life.

The main points:

- Zacchaeus was a tax collector who kept money for himself and acted in a selfish and dishonest way.
- Jesus was visiting his village with a large crowd, so Zacchaeus climbed a tree to get a good view.
- Despite the crowd Jesus saw Zacchaeus, had a meal with him, and Jesus forgave him.
- Zacchaeus was a changed man.

Discussion

Ask the children why they think Jesus forgave Zacchaeus. What evidence was there that Zacchaeus had changed? Link the discussion of Zacchaeus with our own situations. We all go wrong and do things which we should not. If we are truly sorry Jesus can take away our guilt and forgive us, wiping the slate clean. If you have the paper from the discussion earlier tear it up as a sign of Jesus taking our wrong things off us and destroying our guilt.

Craft

You will need:

- paper, pens and pencils

Give each child a piece of paper and ask them to draw four expressions of Zacchaeus from the story:

- feeling sad because everyone hated him
- angry at having to climb the tree
- puzzled at Jesus noticing him
- happy after being forgiven by Jesus

Memory chant

Learn this chant this week:

Whatever we've done, wherever we've been,
Jesus' forgiveness makes us clean!

Prayer

Light a candle in the middle of the room with the children sitting around it in a circle. Ask the children to sit quietly for two minutes, looking at the candle and thinking of the things in their own lives that Jesus needs to forgive.

Songs

Jesus' love is a powerful love
God is good, we sing and shout it
Jesus' love is very wonderful
Thank you, Lord
God loves you, he cares about you

Chant

Whatever we've done, wherever we've been, Jesus' forgiveness makes us clean!

Draw a picture here →

Zacchaeus climbs a Tree

CHANGED!

Unravel the words and ✦ fill the gaps: ✦

Zacchaeus [detnaw] to see Jesus but he was too [slalm]. He climbed a [reet], but [useJs] noticed him. Zacchaeus met with Jesus [nad] he was [gancehd].

Write here the things you do wrong ↘

"sorry, Jesus."

Session 5   Jesus and . . . the people around us __

Theme   There is no one who is unimportant or worthless to Jesus. Jesus cares for all sorts of people – so should we.

Game   *What do I do?*
Children take it in turn to act out or mime the following jobs and pastimes in front of the rest of the group. The other children try to guess what they are. It may help for you to have cards with the answers written on to hold up when they have guessed correctly.

Pop star	Motorbike rider
Footballer	Woodworker/Carpenter
Fishing	Cricketer
Sewing	Mountain climber
Swimming	Teacher

Discussion
- Which of those activities do the children enjoy doing?
- Which of them would they like to spend a day doing?
- Which person would they like to be their best friend?

There are some people who we like to go around with and others who we do not. Friendships are often based on what we enjoy doing together as well as personalities. For instance, the Queen is not likely to go out to tea with your teacher – she will have her own friends to spend time with. Ask the children if they know what types of people Jesus went around with and spent time with.

Active game   *Anagrams*
Show the children cards with the following anagrams. As each one is guessed they should all walk around the room pretending to be the sort of person described by the word. Write the answers on the back of the cards so that they can be pinned up to remind the children:

RCIH (rich)	CKIS (sick)
CEVERL (clever)	DLO (old)
ROPO (poor)	GOUNY (young)
DETHA (hated)	DAS (sad)
DLIBN (blind)	MEAL (lame)

Jesus did not just go around with one type of person. He wanted to talk to everyone and help everyone.

31

Craft

You will need:

- scissors
- glue
- old newspapers and magazines
- large sheet of paper

Work together with all the children making a huge collage of people – young and old, happy and sad, and so on, cutting their pictures from the papers and magazines.

Bible input

Luke 17:11-19

The healing of the ten lepers

Explain the attitude to those with skin diseases like leprosy at the time of Jesus. Mention how they had to shout to warn people to move out of their way, and how hurt they must have felt to be shunned by everyone else in their communities.

Read the account from the Bible, with children acting out the parts of Jesus and the ten lepers. Remember to use a child-friendly translation (Good News/Contemporary English Version/International Children's Bible) or a story Bible.

Quiz

Split the children into two groups with a leader in each. The leader should have a piece of paper and pen. Ask the following questions one by one, giving time for the group to decide quietly on the answer and write it down. At the end collect in the two papers and compare answers. The winning group is the one with the most correct answers:

Q. Where was Jesus going to?
A. *Jerusalem*

Q. How many lepers were there?
A. *Ten*

Q. What happened when lepers approached others?
A. *They moved away*

Q. Who did Jesus tell them to go to see?
A. *Priests*

Q. How many went back to see Jesus?
A. *One*

Q. What did the man say to Jesus?
A. *Thank you*

Talk and discussion

- Ask the children how they would have felt if they had really been the lepers mentioned in the story.

- Jesus helped the lepers even though most people hated and feared them.

- Jesus showed his love to all people, whatever their background and whatever they were suffering with.

- It seems sad that only one leper bothered to return to say 'thank you' to Jesus.

Jesus gives us an example of how we should treat the people around us. We should go out of our way to care for them even if other people can't be bothered. Invite the children to make suggestions of people or situations where they could help people who are modern 'outcasts'.

Memory chant

Learn this chant this time:

Jesus cares for me and you;
we should care for others too.

Prayer

Ask all the children to shout out names at the appropriate times:

My name is . . .
Thank you, Jesus, that you care for me.
My brothers and sisters are . . .
Thank you, Jesus, that you care for them.
My friends are . . .
Thank you, Jesus, that you care for them.
Thank you, Jesus, that you care for the people around us.
Amen

Songs

God is our father
Have you seen the pussy cat?
I am a lighthouse
Jesus, Jesus, here I am

More information

It may be worth contacting a mission or aid agency such as the Leprosy Mission to find out about the problems caused by leprosy today.

5. Jesus and ... the people around us.

TEN things that I enjoy doing...

1
2
3
4
5
6
7
8
9
10

TEN LEPERS

Number the pictures in the correct order

Help! They ask Jesus to help.

One turns back towards Jesus.
Joy Thank you.

Jesus tells them to go to their priests.
GO TO THE PRIESTS

... and go away happy.
Joy! Joy!

Ten Lepers walk along.

They realise that they are healed...

Jesus Sees them

Jesus asks...
Where are the others?

Chant

Jesus cares for me and you, we should care for others too.

Session 6   Jesus and . . . the people who hurt us

Theme

We all get hurt by others. Jesus has forgiven us, so we should forgive those who hurt us and cause us pain.

Game

And and but

Ask for a volunteer. The child must talk to you and answer your questions for one minute without saying 'and' or 'but'. If they do they are out of the game straight away and another child has a go. Repeat this with some or all of the group depending on time.

Talk

In that game, if someone made a mistake they were automatically out of the game, and there was no way back in. There was no chance of 'forgiveness'. This is what we learned in Session 4 – Jesus forgives, even though there should be no way back for us.

Story and activity

Read this story, stopping at the appropriate points to ask, 'What would you have done?' and allowing some of the children to make suggestions.

Steve and Ben were both in the same class at school. They lived in the same town and in the same street. They walked along the same road to school at the same time each day. They supported the same football team, liked the same music, and watched the same TV programmes. They were very good friends, and played together each night after school.

Now, one day Ben was excited. It was nearly his birthday and he really really wanted a new bike. On the day itself his mum said he could go out on his new, shiny bike after school.

When school ended Steve and Ben dashed out as fast as they could. They ran across the playground, through the gates, tore down the road and turned onto their street, puffing and panting. In no time Ben and Steve had got changed and were ready to go off cycling, Steve on his old battered bike and Ben on his shiny new one.

They raced around the park, but Ben won time and time again – Steve's chain kept coming off. Steve asked for a go on the new bike, but Ben refused.

What would you have done?

Then Ben had to go home to have a birthday tea with his family and Steve was left sitting on his bike wondering what to do. As he sat there a bad idea crept into his head. 'Why don't I just borrow Ben's bike for a few minutes?' he thought, looking at the sparkling new bike leaning on the wall. 'No one will know.'

What would you have done?

Steve got off his bike and quietly sneaked up to Ben's house, wheeling the bike away and jumping on as he pushed it into the road. It was as smooth, as fast and as great to ride as he had imagined. He rode down the road and, turning the corner, lost control on some oil. The bike swung from under him and shot over the road into the path of a car. The driver slammed on his brakes but it was too late – the front wheel was squashed.

What would you have done?

As Steve got up and dusted himself down he looked over and was horrified. He was nearly in tears as he took the bike back to Ben's house and faced his angry mum, and saw how much he had upset his friend. But Ben was really good about it.

What would you have done?

'I know it was an accident' he said. 'I'll soon get it mended and then I'll be able to ride it again.' Steve went home feeling a little happier, and the next day they were as good friends as they had always been.

Only a few days later, when Ben and Steve were playing football with Steve's new ball, Ben kicked it onto the railway line. There was no way they could get it back.

What would you have done?

Steve was furious with Ben, stormed off, and would not even speak to him the next day at school. Ben thought that was unfair, especially after Steve had ruined his new bike.

What would you have done?

Discussion

Discuss with the children how Steve and Ben acted in the story. Ask and answer the following questions:

- Was what Ben did in forgiving Steve right or wrong?

- Was Steve right to borrow the bike without asking?

- Should Steve have forgiven Ben after the ball was lost?

Bible input

John 18:15-18, 25-27; 21:15-19

Peter's denial, Jesus' forgiveness

Briefly retell these stories, emphasising the way that Peter said he did not know his best friend, Jesus, three times, and the way that, despite those denials, Jesus still forgave him.

Talk Jesus had been hurt by Peter's denial, yet he did not let it destroy his friendship.

- It can be very hard to forgive, and it takes strength and courage to do so.

- We all hurt and upset people in similar ways to Ben and Steve.

- Jesus sets us the right example – even though he was hurt he still forgave.

Memory chant Learn this one this time:

Jesus shows the way to be
when someone has upset me.

Prayer Ask the children to pray silently while some quiet music plays. Invite them to ask God to help them forgive others when they do things that hurt them.

Songs God is our father
Jesus' love is a powerful love
Father God
If I've upset you, my brother
God loves you, he cares about you

6. Jesus and... the people who hurt us.

BEN and STEVE

Ben sees his bike after the accident, but he forgives Steve.

Steve is angry with Ben for losing his ball.

fill in what they say.

Why do you think God forgives?

Chant Jesus shows the way to be, when someone has upset me.

Session 7   Jesus and . . . prayer _____

Theme   To keep any friendship or relationship going we need to communicate. To maintain our friendship with Jesus we need to talk to him.

Active game   *Captain's aboard*
Assign different areas of the room to be port, starboard, forward and aft. When these names are called out the children have to run to the appropriate area. The last child to get there is out of the game. Further actions and instructions can be added such as:

Captain's aboard	*stand and salute*
Scrub the decks	*mime this action*
Climb the rigging	*mime this action*
Attend the lifeboats	*give someone a 'piggyback'*

Discussion   Bring out the point that when playing 'Captain's Aboard' we all needed to listen and act. Sometimes we have to listen very carefully to hear what messages are being given to us.

Ask the children to name as many different ways of sending and receiving messages as possible. They should include the following:

Telephone	Fax
Internet	E-mail
Talking	Letter
Newspaper	Message through someone else

Quiz   Divide the children into at least two teams. Read out the following clues for different types of people that the children might talk to at some time. There are three clues per person. Award three points to a team if they guess the answer after the first clue, two points if they guess after the second clue, and one point if they guess after the third clue.

Mum/Dad/Main carer

  1. They cook your food
  2. They usually live with you
  3. They write notes to school about you

Teacher

  1. You see them most days, but not at weekends

2. They work in buildings full of children

3. Each class has one

Friends

1. You probably have some here

2. They are not your relatives

3. You play with them

Shopkeeper

1. You give them money

2. Many work in town centres

3. They sell things

Game

Chinese whispers

Arrange at least six children in a line. Whisper a message to the first person and pass it along the line to the other end. Then see what the final message is and how it differs from the original.

Craft

You will need:

• card templates of a speech bubble

• card

• pens and pencils

Allow each child to make at least three speech bubbles. Then ask them to write on the bubbles the kind of things Jesus said to others. They will need some help with this, so be prepared for their questions. Jesus used phrases like:

• Your faith has made you well

• Love the Lord

• You will be better if you believe

• Go – you're forgiven

• Do not worry

• Trust me

• If you've seen me you've seen God

Discussion

Continue the theme of the craft and Session 5, thinking about the types of people Jesus talked to. He talked to his family, friends, the lonely, the powerful, the rich, and so on. But he spoke most of all to his Father God.

Talk about the different people the children talk to. Remind them that it is important to talk to others – then relationships grow.

Bible input

Luke 22:39-46

Jesus prays before he is arrested

Explain that Jesus was about to be arrested, beaten and finally hung on a rough cross. Yet he wanted to talk to his Father about these things, so he made time away from others to pray and talk. At other times he used to thank God or ask him to help others, but this time he wanted help for what was going to happen to himself.

Read out the passage, and explain that the 'cup of suffering' was his imminent suffering and death. But he knew what his Father wanted and he went ahead with it.

God is interested in hearing us talk to him, whatever we or others need. We should be able to talk to God about everything – he knows how we feel.

Memory chant

Learn this chant this time:

Whatever we need, whatever we fear
we can talk to God – he'll always hear.

Prayer

Use a teaspoon to help in your prayers. Explain to the children that three of the main letters in the word teaspoon are T, S and P. Then lead them in prayers under these headings:

Thank you – for friends, for family, for people we can talk to.

Sorry – for the things we do wrong, for the hurtful things we say.

Please – help us to talk to you more, help others in need.

Songs

Thank you, Lord
Jesus, Jesus
God has got a plan
Lord, you put a tongue in my mouth
My God is so big

Communication

Join up the wires.

Jesus Prays

"I don't want to do this"

"Give me more money"

"Take this cup of suffering away from me"

"I'm hungry"

"I'll do what you want, Father God"

"Not my will, but yours"

Put a circle around the things that Jesus prayed ☼ before he was ☼ arrested (LUKE 22:39-46)

Write a 'Thank You' prayer here:

Dear Jesus,
Thank you ———

Chant

Whatever we need, whatever we fear, we can talk to God, He'll always hear!

Session 8   Jesus and . . . the Bible _____

Theme   The Bible is a guide for all of us to follow. It helps us find the right way through life. Jesus used it (he only had the Old Testament, of course) and so should we.

Quiz   *Hangman*

Divide the children into two teams which take it in turns to guess the letters. They could score points for each correct word guessed, or only for guessing the whole Bible verse. Use the following verse (Psalm 119:105):

> Your word is a lamp to guide me
> and a light to my path.

You may find it easier if you have the verse written out on a piece of paper to consult while you fill in the letters.

Talk   The writer of this psalm (poem) saw the word of the Bible as a light to guide and a lamp to show the way. Jesus read the Psalms and a few other parts of the Bible that we now call the Old Testament, and based much of what he said on psalms like this one.

- A light that shines in a dark room reveals things and shows what is there.

- At night we can see where we are going if there are street lights or if we take a torch.

- The Bible helps us to see where we should be going in life.

Game   Blindfold three children. Ask them to imagine that it is late at night and the lights have just gone off in the room. Give each child three of the following items to identify:

vase	mug	blunt scissors
teapot	watering can	CD or tape
badge	toy car	spanner

When the game is over ask them how it was to try to do it in the dark, making the point that it is much easier to do things in the light.

Craft   You will need:

- a roll of old wallpaper
- pens and pencils
- scissors

Explain that before books were invented writings were on scrolls. Jesus would have used bits from the Bible, but read them on scrolls made of animal skins, papyrus or parchment. Give each child a length of the wallpaper at least 100 cm long. Show them how to roll it up like a scroll, and write on it 'God's word is a light', decorating it with relevant pictures.

Bible input   Luke 4:16-21

Jesus reads from Isaiah

Read out the passage. Afterwards explain that even in his home town the people didn't realise how special he was. It was usual for people to be allowed to speak in the synagogue, and rather than saying his own words or giving a speech or sermon Jesus read from the Bible – God's word, which he knew and understood. The people were confused when Jesus said that they had seen the prophecy become reality there and then! He had set those listening an example – it was and is important to read the Bible and think about what it says to us.

Then read out the passage again, asking the children to imagine the scene.

You may want to mention some other times when Jesus referred to the scriptures:

- when he was tempted (Luke 4:1-13)
- with the rich young man (Mark 10:17-22)
- in the Temple as a boy (Luke 2:41-51)

Discussion   Ask the children what different types of books they know and use. Consider what each type of book does and does not show. It may be useful to have a range of books available such as the ones here:

Road Atlas – shows where you should be going and helps you plan a journey

Story book – to entertain and often to give a message too

History book – tells you what happened in the past

Song book – gives us words and tunes to enjoy

Dictionary – helps us find out the meaning of words

Encyclopaedia – helps us find out more about things that interest us

Poetry book – gives us words to enjoy and things to think about
Adventure stories – exciting things to imagine and enjoy

Explain to the children that the Bible contains examples of all the books listed in some form. Whatever type of book we enjoy there is some of it in the Bible. But the Bible is like any other book – it is no good to us unless we read it!

Talk about what the word 'bible' means (a collection of books, 66 in this case!) and how to read the Bible (start with a Gospel, do not start at the front). You may also want to give out Bible notes which will help the children get to grips with the Bible and learn to use it.

Memory chant

Learn this one this session:

The Bible shows us all the way;
it's great to read it every day.

Prayer

Explain and teach the children the response 'God's love is eternal' and then use Psalm 136:1-9, 26 (preferably from the Good News version of the Bible) as a prayer.

Songs

Don't build your house on the sandy land
God's way (Take the Bible)
God has got a plan
Get up out of bed

Further information

Children's Bible notes are available from Christian bookshops or direct from the publishers. Publishers of dated and undated material include:

Scripture Union

Bible Reading Fellowship

CWR

8. Jesus and... the Bible.

The Bible.

Tick the things that are in the Bible:

* Poems and love stories ☐

* Adventures ☐

* History and battles ☐

* Stories of Jesus ☐

* Good help and advice ☐

Bible Bits

Look at the index of a Bible and number these in the correct order:

Chant

The Bible shows us all the way, it's great to read it every day!

Try to find some **Bible** notes and read the **Bible** yourself.

Session 9   Jesus and . . . the Church _____

Theme   Jesus thought it was important to attend a place of worship (the synagogue/the Temple). It is important for all people who trust Jesus to meet with others.

Active game   *Living statues*
Divide the children into several groups. They must arrange themselves to depict the following scenes within a given time. Then, when you clap or blow a whistle, they must freeze like statues. Some children may need to 'act' inanimate objects such as netball posts or bus seats. Suggested scenes:

A netball match	A trip to the zoo
A disco or party	School at playtime
A bus ride	Sports day

Craft   You will need:

- paper
- pens and pencils

First ask the children to draw and colour in their idea of what a church is on one side of the paper. Don't be surprised if there are lots of spires and dull churchyards. Then explain to the children that the 'church' is not the building but all the different people who attend. On the other side of the paper they should then draw and colour all kinds of people – small, tall, young, old, happy, sad, well, ill, and so on.

Discussion   Ask the children about the game. Would it have worked if all the children had done their own thing and not worked as a team? No one could have completed the scenes on their own. Then talk about the things it is fun to do with others, such as playing football and netball. It would be really boring to watch *Neighbours* or another TV show if there was only one character in it.

Find out from the children what teams or groups they belong to. This may include sports teams, clubs, cubs or brownies. If we are part of a team we work together and help each other.

Game   *My team*
Invite a child to come out to the front and talk for 30 seconds about a team or group they belong to. If they stop before the time is up they are out of the game. Repeat this with as many of the children as possible – it is surprisingly difficult!

Talk and Bible input

Luke 2:41-51

The boy Jesus in the Temple

Jesus was part of a team, with his disciples helping him and being his friends. One thing they always did was go to the synagogue (church) together and join the others who wanted to talk to, sing to and worship God. Jesus had been going to the synagogue to worship ever since he was a little boy because his parents, Mary and Joseph, had always taken him and thought it was important to go. Jesus even spent time there when he didn't have to.

Read the passage, explaining that, once a year, a large number of people would gather to go to the Temple in Jerusalem and worship there. Narrate the story while all the children act it out as the crowd, Mary and Joseph, priests in the Temple, and Jesus. If possible follow this pattern:

- Start outside, rushing to get to the Temple in time
- Once inside, aim for the Temple, where all worship
- The crowd leave and slowly head home
- Mary and Joseph realise that Jesus is missing
- Jesus stays, talking to the priests in the Temple
- Mary and Joseph eventually find him there
- Jesus explains that he wanted to be in God the Father's house

Bring out the fact that Jesus enjoyed being in the place where he could learn more about God and worship him. It is good for us to learn more, and to spend time with others praying and singing to God. This can happen in the group and in churches.

Memory chant

Learn this one this time:

To grow we know just what to do,
sing and learn with others too.

Prayer

Sit in a circle and look at each other. Go around the circle and say each other's names. Then pray this prayer, which you may want to write out so that the children can join in:

Thank you, Jesus, for all of us here.
Thank you that we can learn about you together.
Thank you that you want us to be together. Amen

Songs

God has got a plan
We will sing together
Be bold, be strong
I hear the sound
Lord, we've come to worship you

Session 10   Jesus and . . . me _____

Theme   Jesus died for everyone. He wants to know each of us personally and be our friend for life.

Game   *Blindfold identity*
Blindfold two or three children at the front. Pick out some of their friends from the group, without telling the blindfolded children who they are. The blindfolded children must identify the others by touching them. Allow only a short time for each identification.

Active game   *You can't be my friend*
Put out sheets of newspaper or small mats on the floor. Play some music, asking the children to move around the room while the music plays. When the music stops they must all stand with both feet completely on the paper. Any who are not able to do this are 'not your friend' and must sit out for the remainder of the game. As the children drop out remove a sheet of paper each time.

Quiz   Obtain photographs or pictures of a number of personalities and celebrities that the children may recognise, number them and put them up on the walls of the room. It may be easiest for you to buy two or three current children/early teens magazines to be in the current 'culture'. The children have to go around with a piece of paper and identify as many as they can. The game could be developed by using pictures of the leaders and children as babies instead of celebrity pictures.

Discussion   Ask the children to think back to the game and talk about how easy it was to identify the people. Some would have been easier than others, and some obvious to some children but not to others. Ask how many children think they know all of the names of those in their:

class   year at school
club   this group

Jesus knows all our names, and he knows all about us. He knows the personalities and celebrities better than we or anyone else does. He knows everything there is to know about us, even if we don't know much about him. But the

59

best thing of all is that he wants us to know him better and he wants us to be his friend for life.

Craft

You will need:

- pens and pencils
- paper

Ask each of the children to draw a self-portrait carefully. Above it they should write *This is me.* Below the self-portrait they should write *Jesus knows all about me*

Bible input

Luke 5:1-11

Jesus invites people to be his friend

Read out this account of what happened from Simon's point of view:

It was just another working day for me and the lads. We were heading in to the shore to sort the boat out and mend a few nets when we saw that man, Jesus, there with a small crowd. I'd never really listened to what he was saying, but loads of people thought he was some sort of messenger from God, or even God himself! I wasn't interested – we'd had a bad night with no fish, and I was tired.

When Jesus came up and asked me to take him out a little way in one of my boats I almost told him to forget it, but something about him made me say 'Yes'. From a short distance Jesus continued talking to the people and telling them lots of clever things which I didn't really understand. Once he'd finished I thought, 'Good, now I can get home', but instead he told me to go further out to where the water was deeper and catch some fish.

By now I was not happy – I am the fisherman, not him! But I thought it was worth a try, and we threw the nets in. Well, they were so full of fish that when we pulled them in the boat almost went over! In a flash I knew Jesus was special and I was not good enough to be near him, let alone be his friend. But Jesus said, 'Come with me as my friend and we'll catch people instead of fish'. I knew I wanted to, and from that day on Jesus was my friend and he changed me completely!

Talk

Bring out the following points:

- Simon thought he wasn't good enough, but we all are.
- Jesus knew what was best for Simon, and he knows what's best for us.
- We can be friends with Jesus now and for the rest of our lives.

Memory chant

Learn this final one:

Jesus wants to be our friend;
his love for us will never end.

Prayer

Invite the children to spend some time thinking about the story of Simon and how Jesus wants all of us to be his friend. Ask the children to listen carefully to this prayer and, if they agree with it, to say 'Amen' at the end:

Thank you, Jesus, that you know everyone and you love us all.
Thank you, Jesus, that you know me and love me.
Help me to be your friend.
Please be my friend. Amen

Songs

Jesus, Jesus
Step by step (Jesus is the living way)
God's not dead
I'm special

Further information

There are a number of booklets available for children who are thinking of being a real friend of Jesus. Look in your local Christian bookshop for details.

JESUS the BEST friend

Name Age friends

Best TV Moods

Parents feelings

Hairs on Head Best Meal sadness

Circle the things your best friend knows about you.

Tick the things that Jesus knows about you.

Chant

Jesus wants to be our friend - His love for us will never end.

Jesus Invites Others

L	B	F	R	I	E	N	D
J	E	S	U	S	Z	C	V
D	U	H	W	L	O	A	Q
S	B	O	A	T	K	T	U
C	A	R	L	C	F	C	A
O	N	E	T	S	F	H	K
M	S	P	E	C	I	A	L
E	D	E	X	O	S	B	O
Y	S	N	I	G	H	T	E

Find 10 words from the story of Jesus and the Fishermen.

JESUS BOAT FISH NETS CATCH SHORE FRIEND SPECIAL COME NIGHT

Cut out and use as a bookmark

Remember: Jesus loves us all.